THE AMAZ

Here are lots of ideas for com
natural wholefood ingredien
savoury dishes which are tasty, healthy and economical.

By the same author
SLIMMING THE VEGETARIAN WAY
VEGAN COOKING

In the same series
BAKING BETTER BREADS
THE BROWN RICE COOKBOOK
INDIAN CURRIES
ITALIAN DISHES
THE MAGIC OF TOFU
ORIENTAL DISHES
PASTA DISHES
PIES, BAKES AND CASSEROLES
PIZZAS AND PANCAKES
QUICHES AND FLANS
SALADS
SIMPLE AND SPEEDY WHOLEFOOD COOKING
VEGETARIAN DINNER PARTIES
THE WHOLEFOOD LUNCH BOX

THE AMAZING AVOCADO

by

LEAH LENEMAN

Illustrated by Ian Jones

THORSONS PUBLISHERS LIMITED
Wellingborough, Northamptonshire

First published 1984

British Library Cataloguing in Publication Data

Leneman, Leah
  The amazing avocado.
  1. Cookery, (Avocado)
  I. Title
  641.6'4653   TX813.A9

ISBN 0-7225-0880-8

Printed in Great Britain by
Richard Clay (The Chaucer Press) Ltd, Bungay, Suffolk

CONTENTS

INTRODUCTION

The avocado is unique. It is a fruit but, unlike other fruits, it can be used for soups, for salads, for savouries and for sweets. Because of its creamy texture and neutral flavour it can form the basis of an incredibly wide variety of dishes. Avocados are still thought of as a luxury but, unlike most foods in that category, they are really good for you, and Britons would benefit from eating a lot more of them.

Avocados have the highest protein content of any fruit (up to 2.3 per cent). They contain no starch, no cholesterol and little or no sugar; and their fat content, being purely vegetable, is beneficial rather than harmful. Avocados also contain variable amounts of minerals and vitamins, including Vitamin A and Vitamin E. Clearly, avocados are an extremely well-balanced food. The main charge against them is that they are 'fattening'. The calorie content of an average avocado is 260 calories. If you were to eat an avocado before a large meal it certainly would not be conducive to slimming, but incorporated sensibly into a wholefood diet, avocados are hardly likely to be a cause of obesity.

In Britain, avocados are sometimes referred to as 'avocado pears' because of their shape. They are in no way related to the pear family and the term is therefore not used in this book. The word 'avocado' originally comes from the Spanish designation '*aguacate*', which was derived from the Aztec word '*ahuacatl*'.

Indigenous to southern Mexico, Colombia and Ecuador, in the fifteenth century the avocado was taken to other parts of the continent by the Incas and Aztecs. The seeds must be replanted very quickly and young seedlings are delicate, which explains why (unlike, say, the pineapple) they were not more widely distributed by the explorers and conquerors of the New World. However, in about 1650 the avocado was introduced in Jamaica; in the latter seventeenth or early eighteen century it reached Cuba, and shortly after 1800 it began to be cultivated in Hawaii.

The great avocado growing areas of the U.S.A. are California and Florida. The first groves were planted in the mid- to late nineteenth century, and from 1900 production began on a commercial scale. Although the avocado was imported from Mexico to southern Europe around 1600, the only Mediterranean country which grows avocados commercially is Israel. For most of the year the bulk of avocados found in Britain and other European countries comes from Israel. In summer Britain imports them mainly from South Africa.

There are numerous different varieties and hybrids of avocados, suitable for different areas and climatic conditions. The commonest found in Britain are the Fuerte, Ettinger, Nabal and Hass. The first two are the traditional green pear shapes, the Nabal is larger and rounder, and the Hass is the small one with the black knobbly skin. Although the fat and water content vary somewhat between them, it would be almost impossible for anyone other than an expert to guess which kind he or she was eating (except that the Hass variety has a more marked flavour than any of the others).

If someone claims to dislike avocados it is usually because they have tried to eat an unripe one. Avocados are unusual in never ripening on the tree, and if eaten while still hard they are quite revolting. To test if an avocado is ripe, hold it in the palm of your hand: it should yield to gentle pressure all over. When avocados are *very* soft then they are best used for dishes in which they are mashed or puréed. If an avocado is not ripe in the shop, then it should be ready for use after two or three days at home (stored at room temperature). Do not store avocados in direct sunlight. If a ripe avocado is not to be used immediately it can be stored in the refrigerator for up to seven days. If only half an avocado is used then the remaining half can be sprinkled with lemon juice, wrapped in cling film, and stored in the refrigerator for a day or two.

Finally, if you plant an avocado stone in a large pot and water it regularly you will never get any avocados off it, but you should end up with a very attractive house plant.

Notes to Recipes
It has not been thought necessary to list 'ripe avocados' in lists of ingredients since no one should *ever* eat an unripe avocado. Similarly, since the stone of an avocado is obviously inedible, recipes in this book rarely include the instruction 'de-stone'; it is understood that when an avocado is sliced the stone will automatically be discarded.

One ingredient which is used in several recipes may be unfamiliar to some readers. Tofu (soya bean curd) is a high-protein low-calorie food which is rapidly growing in popularity. The most easily obtainable variety is *Morinaga Silken Tofu*, stocked by most health food stores. However, silken tofu is very soft and is therefore suitable only for certain recipes. Firm tofu is available through some wholefood shops and Chinese shops, or it can be made at home — see my book, *Vegan Cooking* (Thorsons, 1982) for instructions.

In theory these recipes are supposed to serve four people, but in practice it depends very much on how they are used: e.g., a dip could be a lunch for two or a party dip for twenty, salad recipes will serve many more as a side dish than as a main dish, and so forth. As a *very* rough guide, a quarter of an avocado per person is about right for a light appetizer or side dish, half an avocado for a more substantial one, and a whole avocado per person for a main dish, though this all still depends very much on the other ingredients, not to mention individual appetites.

Vegan Alternatives to Dairy Ingredients

Milk — There are several soya milks available at health food stores, in cartons, tins and powdered form. Any of these may be used in place of dairy milk.

Cream — There are two soya creams currently on the market; alternatively, undiluted tinned soya milk, or double-strength powdered soya milk may be used. (In some recipes in this book that is termed 'rich soya milk'.) For whipped cream, at time of writing, in Britain,

Snowcrest, Tesco and Waitrose all produce vegan imitation creams which can be whipped.

Vegetable Margarine — Most vegetable margarines contain dairy derivatives, but there are a few which do not, the most readily available being *Tomor* and *Vitaquell*.

Yogurt — By following the instructions on dried yogurt ferments (available at health food stores), soya yogurt can be made using any soya milk. (The milk should always be boiled first and then cooled to lukewarm.) The soya yogurt itself can then be used as a starter for further batches. The yogurt can be made thicker by diluting tinned soya milk with less water or by adding a greater proportion of powdered soya milk to water than the instructions advise.

Cottage Cheese — Drain firm tofu well. Mix in some soya yogurt and a little salt.

Cream Cheese — Pour thick soya yogurt into a large piece of muslin. Tie up and leave to hang overnight.

Scrambled Tofu — Mash firm tofu with a sprinkling of turmeric and a little soya sauce. Fry in a little margarine or vegetable oil, turning frequently until beginning to brown.

1.
AVOCADO SOUPS

AVOCADO AND CASHEW SOUP

Imperial (Metric)
3 oz (75g) cashews
1 large avocado
²/₃ pint (340ml) water
1 teaspoonful oregano
Sea salt to taste

American
¾ cupful cashews
1 large avocado
1½ cupsful water
1 teaspoonful oregano
Sea salt to taste

1. Grind the cashews finely. Add the water and liquidize.

2. Peel and dice the avocado. Add to the liquidizer, along with
    seasonings, and liquidize well.

3. Pour into a saucepan and heat until just below simmer point.

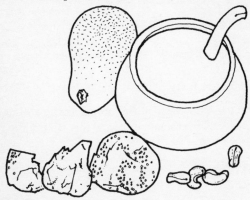

CHILLED AVOCADO AND TOMATO SOUP 1

Imperial (Metric)
2 tomatoes
1 small onion
1/2 small green pepper
1 large avocado
1 pint (570ml) tomato juice
1 dessertspoonful lemon juice

American
1 tomato
1 small onion
1/2 small green pepper
1 large avocado
2 1/2 cupfuls tomato juice
2 teaspoonsful lemon juice

1. Peel and chop the tomatoes. Quarter the onion. Dice the green pepper. Peel and dice the avocado.

2. Pour the tomato and lemon juice into the liquidizer, add rest of ingredients and liquidize well.

3. Chill before serving.

CHILLED AVOCADO AND TOMATO SOUP 2

Imperial (Metric)
1 small onion
1 small clove garlic
1 avocado
Juice of 1/2 lemon
1 pint (570ml) tomato juice
Sea salt and freshly ground black
   pepper to taste
2 tablespoonsful minced parsley

American
1 small onion
1 small clove garlic
1 avocado
Juice of 1/2 lemon
2 1/2 cupsful tomato juice
Sea salt and freshly ground black
   pepper to taste
2 tablespoonsful minced parsley

1. Grate the onion finely. Crush the garlic.

2. Mash the avocado. Beat in the onion, garlic and lemon juice. Gradually stir in the tomato juice and mix well, adding seasoning to taste.

3. Chill before serving, topped with parsley.

LEMONY AVOCADO SOUP

Imperial (Metric)	American
1 large onion	1 large onion
1 clove garlic	1 clove garlic
4 tablespoonsful vegetable oil	4 tablespoonsful vegetable oil
2 tablespoonsful wholemeal flour	2 tablespoonsful wholewheat flour
2 avocados	2 avocados
1 pint (570ml) water	2½ cupsful water
½ vegetable stock cube	½ vegetable stock cube
Grated rind and juice ½ lemon	Grated rind and juice ½ lemon
2 tablespoonsful minced parsley	2 tablespoonsful minced parsley

1. Mince the onion and garlic. Sauté in the oil until tender.

2. Stir in the flour and mix well.

3. Mash the avocados and add to the saucepan.

4. Gradually stir in the water, stock cube, juice and rind of lemon.

5. Heat just to simmer point.

6. Serve topped with parsley.

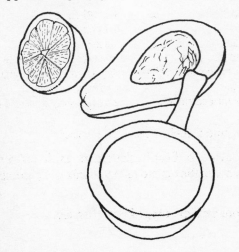

AVOCADO VEGETABLE SOUP

Imperial (Metric)	American
1 carrot	1 carrot
2 sticks celery	2 stalks celery
1 spring onion	1 scallion
4 tomatoes	2 tomatoes
1 avocado	1 avocado
¾ pint (425ml) water	2 cupsful water
¾ pint (425ml) tomato juice	2 cupsful tomato juice
1 teaspoonful mixed herbs	1 teaspoonful mixed herbs
Sea salt to taste	Sea salt to taste

1. Mince the carrot, celery and spring onion (scallion). Peel and chop the tomatoes.

2. Peel and dice the avocado.

3. Place all the ingredients in the liquidizer and liquidize thoroughly.

4. Pour into a saucepan and heat gently just to simmer point.

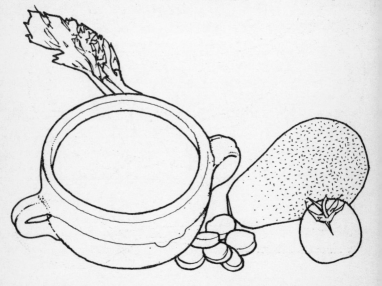

CHILLED AVOCADO AND YOGURT SOUP

Imperial (Metric)
2 large avocados
Juice of 1 lemon
2 teaspoonsful vegetable oil
½ pint (285ml) yogurt *or* soya
    yogurt (page 10)
Sea salt to taste

American
2 large avocados
Juice of 1 lemon
2 teaspoonsful vegetable oil
1⅓ cupsful yogurt *or* soy yogurt
    (page 10)
Sea salt to taste

1. Peel the avocados and mash. Beat in the rest of the ingredients or, alternatively, put everything in a liquidizer and blend thoroughly. Chill.

HOT AVOCADO AND YOGURT SOUP

Imperial (Metric)
1 onion
1 clove garlic
4 tablespoonsful vegetable oil
2 avocados
1 pint (570ml) water
½ vegetable stock cube
2 tablespoonsful wholemeal flour
¼ pint (140ml) yogurt *or* soya
   yogurt (page 10)
Grated rind and juice of 1 lemon
2 tablespoonsful minced parsley

American
1 onion
1 clove garlic
4 tablespoonsful vegetable oil
2 avocados
2½ cupsful water
½ vegetable stock cube
2 tablespoonsful wholewheat flour
⅔ cupful yogurt *or* soy yogurt
   (page 10)
Grated rind and juice of 1 lemon
2 tablespoonsful minced parsley

1. Chop the onion finely. Mince the garlic.

2. Heat the oil in a saucepan and sauté the onion and garlic until tender.

3. Peel and mash the avocados, then add the pulp to the saucepan.

4. Add the water and stock cube and heat gently until just below simmering point.

5. Mix the flour with the yogurt and add to the saucepan along with the lemon rind and juice, stirring well.

6. Continue stirring over a gentle heat until soup has thickened slightly.

7. Sprinkle with parsley before serving.

CURRIED AVOCADO SOUP

Imperial (Metric)
2 avocados
2 teaspoonsful curry powder
¼ pint (140ml) cream *or* rich soya milk (page 9)
Juice of 1 lemon
1 pint (570ml) water
½ vegetable stock cube
Sea salt and freshly ground black pepper
2 tablespoonsful minced parsley

American
2 avocados
2 teaspoonsful curry powder
⅔ cupful cream *or* rich soy milk (page 9)
Juice of 1 lemon
2½ cupsful water
½ vegetable stock cube
Sea salt and freshly ground black pepper
2 tablespoonsful minced parsley

1. Peel the avocados and put the flesh into a liquidizer.

2. Add the curry powder, cream and lemon juice and liquidize.

3. Heat the water to boiling point and pour half of it into the liquidizer, along with the ½ vegetable stock cube. Liquidize again.

4. Add the avocado mixture to the remainder of the hot water in a saucepan and stir over gentle heat until mixture is warmed through. Taste and season.

5. Sprinkle with parsley before serving.

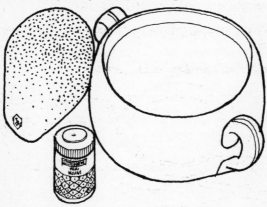

AVOCADO VICHYSSOISE

Imperial (Metric)	**American**
3 leeks	3 leeks
1 large onion	1 large onion
2 tablespoonful vegetable margarine	2 tablespoonful vegetable margarine
1 lb (450g) potatoes	1 pound potatoes
1½ pints (850ml) water	3¾ cupsful water
½ vegetable stock cube	½ vegetable stock cube
1 avocado	1 avocado
¼ pint (140ml) cream *or* rich soya milk (page 9)	⅔ cupful cream *or* rich soy milk (page 9)
¼ teaspoonful freshly grated nutmeg	¼ teaspoonful freshly grated nutmeg
Sea salt to taste	Sea salt to taste
Sprinkling of paprika	Sprinkling of paprika

1. Chop the leeks and onion. Sauté for 3-4 minutes in the margarine.

2. Peel and slice the potatoes thinly. Add to the leek and onion.

3. Pour in the water and add the stock cube. Bring to the boil, then cover and simmer for about 15 minutes until tender. Set aside to cool.

4. Peel and chop the avocado. Place in liquidizer and add the leek and potato mixture and the cream or rich soya milk. Also add the nutmeg and salt. Liquidize thoroughly.

5. Place in refrigerator until thoroughly chilled. Sprinkle with paprika before serving.

2.

DIPS AND SPREADS

Guacamole is a generic name for a spicy avocado dip or spread, originating in Mexico. Here are recipes for three variations, though there are many more permutations.

GUACAMOLE 1

Imperial (Metric)	American
2 avocados	2 avocados
1 onion	1 onion
1 clove garlic	1 clove garlic
Juice of 1 lemon	Juice of 1 lemon
1 tablespoonful olive oil	1 tablespoonful olive oil

1. Mince (or grate) the onion finely. Crush the garlic.

2. Mash the avocados well. Add the rest of the ingredients and mix thoroughly.

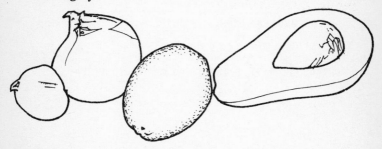

GUACAMOLE 2

Imperial (Metric)
2 avocados
1 teaspoonful grated onion
1 teaspoonful lemon juice
1 dessertspoonful olive oil
Tabasco sauce, cayenne *or* chilli
   powder to taste
Dash of sea salt

American
2 avocados
.1 teaspoonful grated onion
1 teaspoonful lemon juice
2 teaspoonsful olive oil
Tabasco sauce, cayenne *or* chili
   powder to taste
Dash of sea salt

1. Mash the avocados well.

2. Combine all the ingredients and beat thoroughly. (Alternatively, this can be done in a liquidizer.)

GUACAMOLE 3

Imperial (Metric)
2 avocados
1 large tomato
1 tablespoonful finely chopped onion
4 tablespoonsful Vinaigrette dressing
   (page 77)
Dash of *Tabasco* sauce
Juice of ½ lemon
Sea salt and freshly ground black
   pepper to taste

American
2 avocados
1 small tomato
1 tablespoonful finely chopped onion
4 tablespoonsful Vinaigrette dressing
   (page 77)
Dash of *Tabasco* sauce
Juice of ½ lemon
Sea salt and freshly ground black
   pepper to taste

1. Mash the avocados well.

2. Peel and chop the tomato finely.

3. Combine all the ingredients and mix thoroughly.

Yogurt (or soya yogurt) may be added to Guacamole to make it creamy. An up-to-date, high-protein variant is to use tofu, as in the two recipes following.

TOFU GUACAMOLE 1

Imperial (Metric)
1 avocado
½ lb (225g) firm tofu *or* 1 carton
   silken tofu
Juice of ½ lemon
2 tablespoonful vegetable oil
1 clove garlic
1 dessertspoonful soya sauce
4 tablespoonsful water

American
1 avocado
1 cupful tofu
Juice of ½ lemon
2 tablespoonsful vegetable oil
1 clove garlic
2 teaspoonsful soy sauce
4 tablespoonsful water

1. Peel and dice the avocado. Crush the garlic.

2. Either mash all the ingredients together or, alternatively, place in a liquidizer and purée.

TOFU GUACAMOLE 2

Imperial (Metric)
½ lb (225g) firm tofu *or* 1 carton
  silken tofu
3 avocados
2 large tomatoes
1 small onion
2 cloves garlic
2 fresh chillies
Juice of ½ lemon
Sea salt to taste

American
1 cupful tofu
3 avocados
2 small tomatoes
1 small onion
2 cloves garlic
2 fresh chilies
Juice of ½ lemon
Sea salt to taste

1. Place the tofu in the liquidizer and purée. Set aside.

2. Peel and dice the tomatoes. Mince the onion, garlic and chillies.

3. Peel and mash the avocados. Add all of the rest of the ingredients and mix thoroughly.

AVOCADO AND CHEESE SPREAD

Imperial (Metric)	American
1 avocado	1 avocado
4 oz (150g) cream cheese *or* soya yogurt cheese (page 10)	½ cupful cream cheese *or* soy yogurt cheese (page 10)
1 clove garlic	1 clove garlic
2 tablespoonsful chopped parsley	2 tablespoonsful chopped parsley
Grated rind and juice of ½ lemon	Grated rind and juice of ½ lemon

1. Peel and mash the avocado. Crush the garlic.

2. Combine all the ingredients, mixing well.

3. Serve on wholemeal toast or crispbreads.

AVOCADO AND BANANA SPREAD

Imperial (Metric)	American
1 avocado	1 avocado
1 dessertspoonful lemon juice	2 teaspoonsful lemon juice
1 small ripe banana	1 small ripe banana
2 tablespoonsful chopped walnuts	2 tablespoonsful chopped English walnuts

1. Peel and mash the avocado and banana.

2. Combine all the ingredients and mix well.

3. Serve as a sandwich spread on wholemeal bread.

AVOCADO, CELERY AND MUSHROOM DIP

Imperial (Metric)
2 sticks celery
2 oz (50g) mushrooms
1 clove garlic
2 avocados
1 dessertspoonful tomato purée
1 teaspoonful mustard
1 dessertspoonful lemon juice
3 tablespoonsful milk *or* soya milk
  (page 9)

American
2 stalks celery
1 cupful mushrooms
1 clove garlic
2 avocados
2 teaspoonsful tomato paste
1 teaspoonful mustard
2 teaspoonsful lemon juice
3 tablespoonsful milk *or* soy milk
  (page 9)

1. Mince the celery and mushrooms. Crush the garlic. Peel and mash the avocados.

2. Combine all the ingredients and mix thoroughly.

NUTTY AVOCADO DIP

Imperial (Metric)
4 spring onions
2 oz (50g) mixed nuts
2 avocados
2 teaspoonsful lemon juice
Pinch sea salt

American
4 scallions
½ cupful mixed nuts
2 avocados
2 teaspoonsful lemon juice
Pinch sea salt

1. Chop the spring onions (scallions). Chop the nuts coarsely. Peel and dice the avocados.

2. Place all the ingredients in liquidizer and blend thoroughly.

CURRIED AVOCADO SPREAD

Imperial (Metric)	American
2 avocados	2 avocados
Juice of 1/2 lemon	Juice of 1/2 lemon
1/2-1 teaspoonful curry powder	1/2-1 teaspoonful curry powder
1 tablespoonful mayonnaise or Sun-O-Life Dressing	1 tablespoonful mayonnaise or eggless mayonnaise
3 tablespoonsful Smokey Snaps	3 tablespoonsful Bakon Bits

1. Mash the avocados.

2. Add the rest of the ingredients and mix thoroughly. (This is nice served on crispbread.)

SAVOURY AVOCADO SPREAD

Imperial (Metric)	American
2 avocados	2 avocados
Juice of 1/2 small lemon	Juice of 1/2 small lemon
2 tomatoes	1 tomato
2 spring onions	2 scallions
2 hard-boiled eggs or 4 oz (115g) scrambled tofu (page 10)	2 hard-boiled eggs or 1/2 cupful scrambled tofu (page 10)
1/4 teaspoonful garlic salt	1/4 teaspoontul garlic salt
Freshly ground black pepper to taste	Freshly ground black pepper to taste

1. Peel and mash the avocados. Mix the lemon juice in well.

2. Peel and chop the tomatoes finely. Mince the spring onions (scallions). Mince the hard-boiled eggs if used.

3. Add the tomatoes, spring onion (scallion) and egg or tofu to the avocado. Mix well and season with garlic salt and black pepper.

4. Cover the bowl and leave to stand in the refrigerator or a cool place for about an hour before serving.

ISRAELI AVOCADO AND AUBERGINE DIP

Imperial (Metric)	American
2 aubergines	2 eggplants
2 spring onions	2 scallions
2 avocados	2 avocados
2 teaspoonsful lemon juice	2 teaspoonsful lemon juice
2 teaspoonsful olive oil	2 teaspoonsful olive oil
1 tablespoonful curry powder	1 tablespoonful curry powder
Sea salt to taste	Sea salt to taste
12 black olives	12 black olives

1. Pierce the aubergine (eggplant) in several spots with a fork. Place in a hot oven 450°F/230°C (Gas Mark 8) until the skins are black and it is soft to the touch.

2. When the aubergine (eggplant) is cool enough to handle, peel the skin off and dice the flesh. Place in a liquidizer.

3. Mince the spring onions (scallions). Add to the liquidizer. Peel the avocados and add the flesh to the liquidizer along with the lemon juice, oil, curry powder and sea salt.

4. Liquidize the mixture thoroughly, stirring in between times to make sure it is thoroughly mixed. Place in a serving dish.

5. Mince the olives and sprinkle over the dip. (This is nice served with pitta bread.)

3.

HOT AVOCADO DISHES

SPICED AVOCADO

Imperial (Metric)	American
2 onions	2 onions
1 clove garlic	1 clove garlic
2 green peppers	2 green peppers
2 small chillies	2 small chilies
4 tablespoonsful olive oil	4 tablespoonsful olive oil
2 tablespoonsful tomato purée	2 tablespoonsful tomato paste
2 tablespoonsful water	2 tablespoonsful water
2 fl oz (60ml) cider vinegar	¼ cupful cider vinegar
4 tablespoonsful *Smokey Snaps*	4 tablespoonsful *Bakon Bits*
4 avocados	4 avocados

1. Mince the onions, garlic, peppers and chillies.

2. Sauté in the olive oil until onions are turning brown. Add the tomato purée (paste), cider vinegar and water. Simmer for about 15 minutes.

3. Peel and dice the avocado.

4. Remove the tomato mixture from the heat and add avocado and *Smokey Snaps* (*Bakon Bits*). Serve at once.

SAN CLEMENTE CURRY

Imperial (Metric)
1 large onion
2 tablespoonsful vegetable
   margarine
1 lb (455g) small mushrooms
2 teaspoonsful (or more to taste)
   curry powder
2 tomatoes
Pinch sea salt
2 dessertspoonsful lemon juice
1/2 pint (285ml) sour cream, yogurt
   or thick soya yogurt (page 10)
4 avocados
Cooked brown rice as required

American
1 large onion
2 tablespoonsful vegetable
   margarine
8 cupsful small mushrooms
2 teaspoonsful curry powder
1 tomato
Pinch sea salt
4 teaspoonsful lemon juice
1 1/3 cupsful sour cream, yogurt or
   thick soy yogurt (page 10)
4 avocados
Cooked brown rice as required

1. Chop the onion. Sauté in the margarine along with the mushrooms until tender.

2. Stir in the curry powder and cook a few moments longer.

3. Chop the tomato and add to the saucepan, along with the salt. Heat through.

4. Add the lemon juice and sour cream or yogurt. Stir well and heat until just below boiling point.

5. Peel and halve the avocados. Place on beds of hot brown rice and fill with the mushroom mixture.

AVOCADO BURGERS

Imperial (Metric)	American
½ lb (225g) soya beans	1 cupful soy beans
2 avocados	2 avocados
1 small onion	1 small onion
2 teaspoonsful prepared mustard	2 teaspoonsful prepared mustard
2 dessertspoonsful tomato purée	4 teaspoonsful tomato paste
Sea salt to taste	Sea salt to taste
Wholemeal breadcrumbs as required	Wholewheat breadcrumbs as required
Vegetable oil as required	Vegetable oil as required

1. Soak and cook the soya beans until tender.

2. Peel and dice the avocado. Chop the onion.

3. Put all the ingredients except the last two into a liquidizer and blend thoroughly.

4. Pour into a mixing bowl and add enough breadcrumbs to be able to form the mixture into burgers.

5. Fry the burgers in vegetable oil until each is brown and crisp on the outside.

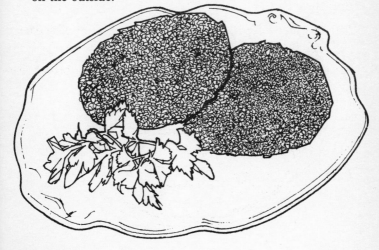

HEATED AVOCADO PURÉE

Imperial (Metric)	American
2 avocados	2 avocados
1 teaspoonful lemon juice	1 teaspoonful lemon juice
Pinch sea salt	Pinch sea salt
Sprinkling of paprika	Sprinkling of paprika
1 teaspoonful grated lemon rind	1 teaspoonful grated lemon rind
1 tablespoonful minced chives *or* spring onion	1 tablespoonful minced chives *or* scallion

1. Peel and mash the avocados.

2. Put them into a saucepan with all the other ingredients. Put the saucepan over a large pan of boiling water (or use a double boiler) and heat the avocado mixture. Serve as a vegetable side dish.

AVOCADO À LA KING

Imperial (Metric)	American
2 oz (50g) vegetable margarine	¼ cupful vegetable margarine
1 oz (30g) wholemeal flour	¼ cupful wholewheat flour
½ pint (285ml) milk *or* soya milk (page 9)	1⅓ cupsful milk *or* soy milk (page 9)
½ lb (225g) mushrooms	4 cupsful mushrooms
2 tinned red pimentos	2 canned red pimentos
2 large avocados	2 large avocados
Sea salt and freshly ground black pepper to taste	Sea salt and freshly ground black pepper to taste
Wholemeal toast, brown rice *or* wholemeal noodles as required	Wholewheat toast, brown rice *or* wholewheat noodles as required

1. Heat half the margarine, add the flour and cook gently for a minute and then gradually add the milk, stirring constantly, to make a white sauce. Set aside.

2. Slice the mushrooms and sauté in the remaining margarine until tender.

3. Chop the pimentos coarsely. Add to the white sauce along with the mushrooms.

4. Peel and dice the avocados. Add to the white sauce just before serving. Season to taste.

5. Serve over toast, rice or noodles.

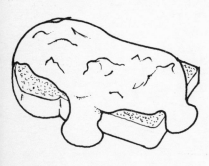

AVOCADOS WITH HOT TOMATO FILLING

Imperial (Metric)	American
½ lb (225g) onions	8 ounces onions
1 large clove garlic	1 large clove garlic
½ lb (225g) tomatoes	8 ounces tomatoes
2 oz (55g) vegetable margarine	¼ cupful vegetable margarine
Sea salt and freshly ground black pepper to taste	Sea salt and freshly ground black pepper to taste
4 small avocados	4 small avocados
1 tablespoonful minced parsley	1 tablespoonful minced parsley

1. Chop the onions finely. Crush the garlic. Skin and slice the tomatoes.

2. Heat the margarine, add onion, garlic and tomatoes, cover and cook slowly until onion is tender, stirring occasionally. Season to taste.

3. Peel and stone the avocados.

4. Pour the tomato mixture over the avocados. Sprinkle with parsley.

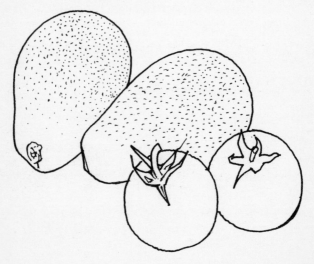

AVOCADO-STUFFED BAKED POTATOES

Imperial (Metric)
1 large avocado
3 oz (85g) cream cheese *or* soya
   yogurt cheese (page 10)
4 baked potatoes

American
1 large avocado
⅓ cupful cream cheese *or* soy
   yogurt cheese (page 10)
4 baked potatoes

1. Peel and mash the avocado.

2. Combine with the cream cheese.

3. Make a cross-cut on the top of the baked potatoes, open and stuff with the avocado mixture.

AVOCADO AND VEGETABLE MÉLANGE

Imperial (Metric)	American
¾ lb (340g) brown rice	2 cupsful brown rice
Small piece of fresh ginger (about ½-inch/1cm)	Small piece of fresh ginger (about ½-inch)
¾ lb (340g) carrots	12 ounces carrots
4 sticks celery	4 stalks celery
½ lb (225g) broccoli	8 ounces broccoli
4 oz (100g) mushrooms	2 cupsful mushrooms
¾ lb (340g) tomatoes	12 ounces tomatoes
4 tablespoonsful vegetable oil	4 tablespoonsful vegetable oil
4 oz (115g) broken walnuts	1 cupful broken English walnuts
4 teaspoonsful honey	4 teaspoonsful honey
4 avocados	4 avocados
Lemon juice as required	Lemon juice as required

1. While preparing the rest of the dish, cook the brown rice until tender.

2. Peel and mince the ginger very finely. Cut the carrots into matchstick pieces. Chop the celery. If the broccoli is the spring purple sprouting kind just use the heads as they are; if it is the green winter kind then chop it finely. Slice the mushrooms. Chop the tomatoes.

3. Heat the oil in a frying pan or a wok and put in the ginger. Then add the rest of the vegetables in the order given, making sure each one is well stirred when added. Add the walnuts.

4. Stir-fry the vegetables until just tender, then sprinkle in the honey.

5. Meanwhile, peel and halve the avocados, remove stones and sprinkle with lemon juice. Place in a moderate oven 350°F/180°C (Gas Mark 4) for a few minutes until just warmed through.

6. Make a bed of rice on four plates. Put the avocados on the rice, then pile the vegetable mixture on top.

NUTTY AVOCADOS

Imperial (Metric)	American
¼ lb (115g) Brazil nuts	1 cupful Brazil nuts
4 tomatoes	2 tomatoes
2 cloves garlic	2 cloves garlic
2 spring onions	2 scallions
2 oz (55g) cashew pieces	½ cupful cashew pieces
2 oz (55g) wholemeal breadcrumbs	1 cupful wholewheat breadcrumbs
4 teaspoonsful tomato purée	4 teaspoonsful tomato paste
Sea salt and freshly ground black pepper	Sea salt and freshly ground black pepper
Few drops *Tabasco* sauce	Few drops *Tabasco* sauce
4 small avocados	4 small avocados
Juice of 1 lemon	Juice of 1 lemon

1. Grind the Brazil nuts finely. Peel and chop the tomatoes. Crush the garlic. Mince the spring onions (scallions).

2. Combine the ground Brazils, the cashew pieces, breadcrumbs, garlic, tomato purée and spring onions (scallions). Mix well. If the mixture is not pleasantly moist then add a few drops of water. Season to taste, adding *Tabasco* sauce as well.

3. Peel, stone and halve the avocados. Brush them well with the lemon juice. Place them on a baking tray.

4. Pile the nut mixture on the avocados. Place in a hot oven 400°F/200°C (Gas Mark 6) for about 10 minutes until heated through.

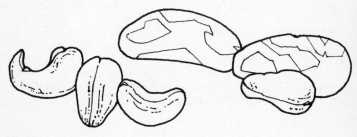

AVOCADO AND MUSHROOM PILAFF

Imperial (Metric)	American
¾ lb (340g) brown rice	2 cupsful brown rice
1 large onion	1 large onion
1 clove garlic	1 clove garlic
4 oz (115g) vegetable margarine	½ cupful vegetable margarine
Sea salt and freshly ground black pepper to taste	Sea salt and freshly ground black pepper to taste
6 oz (170g) mushrooms	3 cupsful mushrooms
6 large tomatoes	4 tomatoes
½ teaspoonful dried oregano	½ teaspoonful dried oregano
2 avocados	2 avocados
1 tablespoonful minced parsley	1 tablespoonful minced parsley

1. Soak the rice overnight or for several hours.

2. Chop the onion and mince the garlic.

3. Melt half the margarine in a saucepan and fry the onion and garlic until golden brown.

4. Drain the rice and add it to the saucepan, stirring well. Add sea salt to taste and enough water to cover the rice. Bring to the boil, turn the heat down to low and simmer until cooked.

5. Meanwhile, slice the mushrooms, and peel and chop the tomatoes.

6. Melt the remainder of the margarine in a frying pan and add the mushrooms. Sauté for 2 or 3 minutes, then add the tomatoes, oregano, sea salt and black pepper and cook for 3 or 4 minutes longer.

7. Peel and dice the avocados. Stir into the tomato and mushrooms mixture.

8. Arrange the rice on a serving dish in a ring and fill the centre with the avocado mixture. Sprinkle the parsley over the top.

AVOCADO AND COTTAGE CHEESE FLAN

Imperial (Metric)	American
2 clove garlic	2 clove garlic
½ pint (285ml) mayonnaise or Sun-O-Life Dressing	1⅓ cupful mayonnaise or eggless mayonnaise
3 avocados	3 avocados
3 oz (85g) cottage cheese plus 3 oz (85g) curd cheese or 6 oz (170g) tofu cottage cheese (page 10)	¾ cupful cottage cheese plus ¾ cupful curd cheese or ¾ cupful tofu cottage cheese (page 10)
1 cooked wholemeal flan case	1 cooked wholewheat flan case
12 black olives	12 black olives

1. Crush the garlic. Add to the mayonnaise.

2. Mash finely half the avocados and mix into the mayonnaise.

3. Combine the cheeses and add about a third of the mayonnaise mixture. Spoon this over the cooked pastry case.

4. Slice the remainder of the avocados and arrange on top of the avocado mayonnaise. Spoon the rest of the avocado mayonnaise over the sliced avocados.

5. Mince the olives and sprinkle over the top.

6. Leave the flan to rest for at least 1 hour before serving. At that stage it can either be heated in the oven at 350°F/180°C (Gas Mark 4) for 10-15 minutes, or alternatively it can be served chilled.

AVOCADO AND YOGURT FLAN

Imperial (Metric)
Uncooked wholemeal flan case
2 spring onions
¼ pint (150ml) natural yogurt,
  soured cream, *or* thick soya
  yogurt (page 10)
Juice of ½ small lemon
Sea salt and freshly ground black
  pepper to taste
2 avocados

American
Uncooked wholewheat flan case
2 scallions
⅓ cupful natural yogurt, sour cream
  or thick soy yogurt (page 10)
Juice of ½ small lemon
Sea salt and freshly ground black
  pepper to taste
2 avocados

1. Prick the bottom of the flan case with a fork in several places. Place it in a fairly hot oven 400°F/200°C (Gas Mark 6) for 15-20 minutes.

2. Meanwhile, mince the spring onions (scallions). Combine the yogurt, spring onions (scallions), lemon juice and seasoning. Mix well.

3. Peel and dice the avocados and fold gently into the yogurt mixture.

4. Remove the flan case from the oven and spoon the avocado mixture into it.

5. Turn the oven heat down to moderate 350°F/180°C (Gas Mark 4) and put the flan back into the oven. Heat through for about 15 minutes before serving.

4.

STUFFED AVOCADO DISHES

In the following recipes the avocado skins are hollowed out and used as 'shells' for the filling.

RAISIN-FILLED AVOCADOS

Imperial (Metric)	American
2 oz (55g) seedless raisins	1/3 cupful seedless raisins
2 avocados	2 avocados
Juice of 1 small lemon	Juice of 1 small lemon
1 dessertspoonful grated onion	2 teaspoonsful grated onion
2 tablespoonsful mayonnaise *or* Sun-O-Life Dressing	2 tablespoonsful mayonnaise *or* eggless mayonnaise
Sea salt, freshly ground black pepper and cayenne to taste	Sea salt, freshly ground black pepper and cayenne to taste

1. Cover the raisins with cold water and bring to the boil. Leave to stand for 5 minutes, drain and dry.

2. Halve the avocados and remove stone. Scoop out the flesh and mash.

3. Add all the rest of the ingredients and mix well.

4. Pile the mixture back into the avocado skins and serve.

SWEETCORN-FILLED AVOCADOS

Imperial (Metric)	American
2 avocados	2 avocados
2 teaspoonsful raw cane sugar	2 teaspoonsful raw cane sugar
2 teaspoonsful mayonnaise *or* Sun-O-Life Dressing	2 teaspoonsful mayonnaise *or* eggless mayonnaise
2 small eating apples	2 small eating apples
2 tablespoonful *Smokey Snaps*	2 tablespoonful *Bakon Bits*
1 medium tin sweetcorn	1 medium can sweetcorn

1. Halve and stone the avocados. Scoop out flesh and put into small mixing bowl.

2. Add the sugar and mayonnaise and whip together with a fork.

3. Peel and grate the apple. Add to mixture, along with *Smokey Snaps* (*Bakon Bits*).

4. Drain the sweetcorn and mix in.

5. Pile the mixture back into the avocado skins and serve.

In the recipes which follow the avocado is peeled, so you would serve it with a knife and fork rather than a spoon.

VEGETABLE-STUFFED AVOCADOS

Imperial (Metric)	American
2 oz (50g) red kidney beans	⅓ cupful red kidney beans
4 oz (115g) fresh or frozen peas	¾ cupful fresh or frozen peas
4 oz (115g) carrots	¾ cupful carrots
4 oz (115g) celery	¾ cupful celery
6 tablespoonsful Vinaigrette Dressing (page 77)	6 tablespoonsful Vinaigrette Dressing (page 77)
4 avocados	4 avocados
Lettuce leaves as required	Lettuce leaves as required
1 tablespoonful minced parsley	1 tablespoonful minced parsley

1. Soak and cook the kidney beans until tender. Cook the peas until tender. Dice the carrot and cook until tender. Cool.

2. Chop the celery. Combine with the beans, peas and carrots.

3. Mix in the vinaigrette. Leave to marinate for several hours.

4. Halve, stone and peel avocados. Place on lettuce leaves.

5. Fill the avocados with the vegetable mixture, sprinkling parsley on top.

ISRAELI AVOCADOS

Imperial (Metric)	American
1 lb (455g) carrots	1 pound carrots
Juice of 3 oranges	Juice of 3 oranges
Juice of 1/2 lemon	Juice of 1/2 lemon
Sea salt to taste	Sea salt to taste
Pinch raw cane sugar	Pinch raw cane sugar
Dash powdered ginger	Dash powdered ginger
4 avocados	4 avocados

1. Coarsely grate the carrots.

2. Pour in the orange and lemon juice, adding salt and sugar to taste, with a dash of powdered ginger. Refrigerate for at least 6 hours. Drain.

3. Peel and halve the avocados. Fill with the carrot mixture.

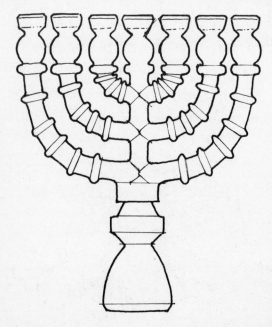

AVOCADOS STUFFED WITH TOMATOES AND MUSHROOMS

Imperial (Metric)	American
½ lb (225g) mushrooms	4 cupsful mushrooms
1 tablespoonful vegetable oil	1 tablespoonful vegetable oil
4 tomatoes	2 tomatoes
2 oz (55g) walnuts	½ cupful English walnuts
2 large avocados	2 large avocados
Juice of ½ lemon	Juice of ½ lemon
2 bunches watercress	2 bunches watercress

1. Chop the mushrooms finely and fry in the oil until tender. Cool.

2. Peel and slice the tomatoes.

3. Combine the tomatoes, mushrooms and walnuts.

4. Peel and halve the avocados. Sprinkle with lemon juice. Place on a bed of watercress.

5. Pile the mushroom mixture in the avocados.

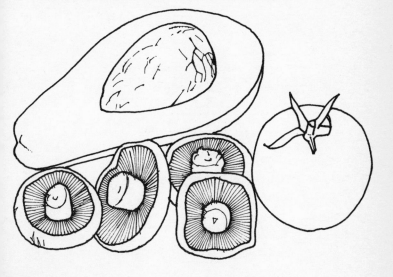

FRUIT-FILLED AVOCADO

Imperial (Metric)	**American**
2 slices fresh pineapple	2 slices fresh pineapple
2 small oranges	2 small oranges
4 tablespoonsful olive oil	4 tablespoonsful olive oil
1 dessertspoonful cider vinegar	2 teaspoonsful cider vinegar
1 teaspoonful lemon juice	1 teaspoonful lemon juice
Sea salt and freshly ground black pepper to taste	Sea salt and freshly ground black pepper to taste
1 teaspoonful raw cane sugar	1 teaspoonful raw cane sugar
2 avocados	2 avocados

1. Cut the peel off the fresh pineapple, dice the pineapple, removing the core.

2. Peel and segment the oranges, then cut the segments in half.

3. Combine oil, vinegar, lemon juice, sugar and seasoning to make a dressing.

4. Combine the fruit and dressing.

5. Peel and halve the avocados. Fill with the fruit mixture.

CREOLE AVOCADOS

Imperial (Metric)	American
2 spring onions	2 scallions
½ small green pepper	½ small green pepper
⅓ pint (200ml) mayonnaise *or* Sun-O-Life Dressing	⅔ cupful mayonnaise *or* eggless mayonnaise
4 tablespoonsful tomato ketchup	4 tablespoonsful tomato catsup
1 dessertspoonful lemon juice	2 teaspoonsful lemon juice
Few drops *Tabasco* sauce	Few drops *Tabasco* sauce
Pinch sea salt	Pinch sea salt
1 lb (455g) firm tofu	2 cupsful firm tofu
4 small avocados	4 small avocados
Lettuce leaves as required	Lettuce leaves as required
2 large tomatoes	2 large tomatoes

1. Mince the spring onions (scallions) and green pepper.

2. Combine the mayonnaise, ketchup, spring onions (scallions), green pepper, lemon juice, *Tabasco* sauce and salt.

3. Cube the tofu and mix with the dressing. Refrigerate for 3 to 4 hours.

4. Halve and peel the avocados. Place on lettuce leaves.

5. Slice the tomatoes and surround the avocados with tomato slices. Fill the avocados with the tofu mixture.

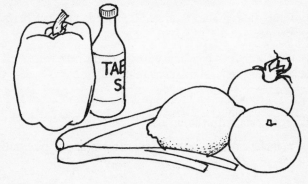

BEAN AND PASTA STUFFED AVOCADOS

Imperial (Metric)	American
4 oz (115g) dried haricot beans	½ cupful dried navy beans
¾ pint (425ml) water	2 cupsful water
6 tablespoonsful olive oil	6 tablespoonsful olive oil
1 bay leaf	1 bay leaf
1 whole clove garlic	1 whole clove garlic
Sea salt to taste	Sea salt to taste
3 tablespoonsful cider vinegar	3 tablespoonsful cider vinegar
2 tablespoonsful minced parsley	2 tablespoonsful minced parsley
½ teaspoonful dried crushed oregano	½ teaspoonful dried crushed oregano
½ teaspoonful dried crushed basil	½ teaspoonful dried crushed basil
¼ teaspoonful dried crushed tarragon	¼ teaspoonful dried crushed tarragon
Sea salt and freshly ground black pepper	Sea salt and freshly ground black pepper
4 oz (115g) wholemeal macaroni	1 cupful wholewheat macaroni
4 small avocados	4 small avocados

1. Soak the beans overnight. Drain and cover with the water. Add half the olive oil and the bay leaf and the clove of garlic. Bring to the boil and simmer until tender, adding the salt toward the end of the cooking time.

2. Drain and discard the garlic clove and bay leaf.

3. Combine the remaining olive oil with the vinegar, herbs, salt and pepper.

4. Place the beans in a bowl and cover with the herb mixture. Cover the bowl and refrigerate overnight.

5. Next day cook the macaroni until tender, drain, cool and chill.

6. Mix the pasta with the beans.

7. Peel and halve the avocados. Fill with the bean and pasta mixture.

5.

AVOCADO AND VEGETABLE SALADS

AVOCADO-STUFFED TOMATOES

Imperial (Metric)
4 'beef' tomatoes (*or* 8 large
  ordinary tomatoes)
2 large avocados
4 sticks celery
½ small onion
2 tablespoonsful olive oil
1 dessertspoonful lemon juice
Pinch sea salt
Pinch cayenne pepper
1 tablespoonful minced parsley

American
4 large tomatoes
2 large avocados
4 stalks celery
½ small onion
2 tablespoonsful olive oil
2 teaspoonsful lemon juice
Pinch sea salt
Pinch cayenne pepper
1 tablespoonful minced parsley

1. Cut each tomato into 4-6 sections, but cut only about ¾ of the way down so that the bottom is intact and the tomatoes can be spread out into a 'flower' shape.

2. Peel and dice the avocados. Mince the celery and onion.

3. Combine the avocado, celery and onion with the olive oil and mix well.

4. Add the lemon juice and seasoning.

5. Pile the avocado mixture onto the tomatoes and sprinkle with parsley.

AVOCADO AND MUSHROOM SALAD

Imperial (Metric)	American
½ lb (225g) mushrooms	4 cupsful mushrooms
1 clove garlic	1 clove garlic
Juice of 2 small lemons	Juice of 2 small lemons
3 fl oz (90ml) olive oil	⅓ cupful olive oil
2 teaspoonsful mustard	2 teaspoonsful mustard
4 medium avocados	4 medium avocados
4 boxes mustard and cress	4 boxes mustard and cress

1. Slice the mushrooms thinly.

2. Crush the garlic and mix with the lemon juice, olive oil and mustard to make a dressing.

3. Combine the mushrooms and dressing and leave to marinate for about ½ hour, turning occasionally.

4. Peel the avocados and slice into long thin pieces.

5. Arrange a bed of cress on four plates and arrange avocado slices on top.

6. Spoon the mushroom mixture over the avocados.

AVOCADO MIXED SALAD

Imperial (Metric)	American
1 tablespoonful vegetable oil	1 tablespoonful vegetable oil
Grated rind and juice of 1 large lemon	Grated rind and juice of 1 large lemon
1 tablespoonful mayonnaise *or* Sun-O-Life Dressing	1 tablespoonful mayonnaise *or* eggless mayonnaise
Sea salt to taste	Sea salt to taste
½ teaspoonful raw cane sugar (optional)	½ teaspoonful raw cane sugar (optional)
2 large tomatoes	2 small tomatoes
1 small leek	1 small leek
1 red pepper	1 red pepper
2 large avocados	2 large avocados
1 lettuce	1 lettuce
1 bunch watercress	1 bunch watercress

1. Combine the oil, lemon juice and rind, mayonnaise, salt and sugar, and set aside.

2. Skin and slice the tomatoes. Thinly slice the leek. De-seed and thinly slice the red pepper. Peel and dice the avocados.

3. Arrange the lettuce leaves on four plates and pile on the above vegetables.

4. Pour the dressing over the salad.

5. Place a border of watercress round the edge of each plate and serve at once.

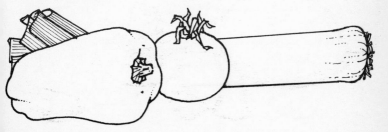

AVOCADO-DRESSED GREEN PEPPER SALAD

Imperial (Metric)	American
1 large avocado	1 large avocado
3 fl oz (90ml) vegetable oil	⅓ cupful vegetable oil
Juice of 1 lemon	Juice of 1 lemon
2 teaspoonful honey	2 teaspoonful honey
2 teaspoonful sea salt	2 teaspoonful sea salt
1 large green pepper	1 large green pepper
4 sticks celery	4 stalks celery
4 spring onions	4 scallions
4 tomatoes	3 tomatoes

1. Peel and dice the avocado.

2. Combine the avocado in a liquidizer with the oil, lemon juice, honey and salt. Liquidize thoroughly and set aside.

3. De-seed and chop the green pepper. Mince the celery and spring onions (scallions). Chop the tomatoes coarsely.

4. Place the chopped vegetables in serving bowl. Pour the avocado mixture over them and mix well.

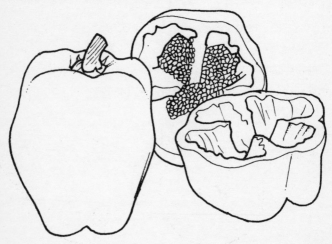

AVOCADO WINTER SALAD

Imperial (Metric)	American
¾ lb (340g) Chinese leaves	12 ounces Chinese cabbage
½ small onion	½ small onion
4 carrots	4 carrots
4 tomatoes	3 tomatoes
1 large avocado	1 large avocado
4 tablespoonsful Vinaigrette Dressing (page 77)	4 tablespoonsful Vinaigrette Dressing (page 77)
2 oz (55g) walnut pieces	½ cupful English walnut pieces

1. Shred the Chinese leaves. Finely mince (or grate) the onion. Cut the carrots into thin sticks. Coarsely chop the tomatoes. Peel and dice the avocado.

2. Combine all of the above vegetables in a bowl. Pour the vinaigrette over and mix thoroughly.

3. Add the walnut pieces and mix again. Serve immediately.

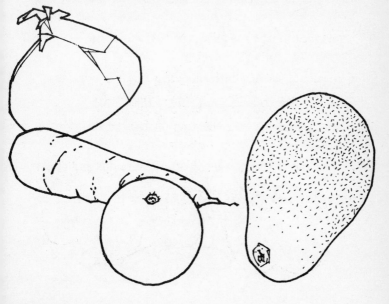

AVOCADO AND NUT SAVOURY SALAD

Imperial (Metric)	**American**
2 tablespoonsful vegetable oil	2 tablespoonsful vegetable oil
1 tablespoonful lemon juice *or* cider vinegar	1 tablespoonful lemon juice *or* cider vinegar
1 teaspoonful dry mustard	1 teaspoonful dry mustard
Pinch each of raw cane sugar, sea salt and freshly ground black pepper	Pinch each of raw cane sugar, sea salt and freshly ground black pepper
½ lb (225g) white cabbage	8 ounces white cabbage
1 medium-sized tin nut savoury (e.g. Granose's *Protose, Nuttolene,* Mapleton's *Luncheon Roll* etc.)	1 medium-sized can nut savoury (e.g. Granose's *Protose, Nuttolene,* Mapleton's *Luncheon Roll* etc.)
2 avocados	2 avocados
2 oz (50g) salted peanuts	3½ tablespoonsful salted peanuts
1 box mustard and cress	1 box mustard and cress

1. Combine the oil, lemon juice and seasoning and beat well. Set aside.

2. Shred the cabbage and make a bed of cabbage on four plates (or one serving dish).

3. Cut the nut savoury into cubes and put it in a bowl.

4. Peel and dice the avocados. Add to the bowl.

5. Pour the dressing over the avocado and nut savoury and mix thoroughly.

6. Pile on top of the cabbage. Top with peanuts and cress.

AVOCADO AND BUTTER BEAN SALAD

Imperial (Metric)	American
1 red pepper	1 red pepper
2 sticks celery	2 stalks celery
½ cucumber	½ cucumber
1 medium carrot	1 medium carrot
3 tablespoonsful olive oil	3 tablespoonsful olive oil
1 tablespoonful lemon juice	1 tablespoonful lemon juice
Sea salt and freshly ground black pepper to taste	Sea salt and freshly ground black pepper to taste
1 large avocado (or 2 small)	1 large avocado (or 2 small)
4 oz (115g) butter beans, soaked and cooked, or 1 × 15 oz (425g) tin butter beans	¾ cupful lima beans, soaked and cooked, or 1 × 15 oz (425g) can lima beans
1 large firm tomato	1 small firm tomato
6 black olives	6 black olives

1. De-seed and slice thinly the red pepper. Slice the celery and cucumber. Grate the carrot coarsely. Mix together.

2. Mix the oil, lemon juice and seasoning together.

3. Peel and dice the avocado. Add to the vegetable mixture, along with the beans.

4. Pour the dressing over and mix thoroughly.

5. Slice the tomato. Mince the olives.

6. Sprinkle the minced olives on top of the salad. Arrange tomato slices in a border round the edge and serve at once.

MACARONI AND AVOCADO SALAD

Imperial (Metric)	American
½ lb (225g) wholemeal macaroni	2 cupsful wholewheat macaroni
2 avocados	2 avocados
Lemon juice as required	Lemon juice as required
1 cucumber	1 cucumber
1 or 2 spring onions	1 or 2 scallions
¼ pint (140ml) mayonnaise *or* Sun-O-Life Dressing	⅓ cupful mayonnaise *or* eggless mayonnaise
2 tablespoonsful minced parsley	2 tablespoonsful minced parsley
1 tablespoonful cider vinegar	1 tablespoonful cider vinegar
1 teaspoonful mustard	1 teaspoonful mustard
½ teaspoonful oregano	½ teaspoonful oregano
Sea salt and freshly ground black pepper to taste	Sea salt and freshly ground black pepper to taste
2 tablespoonsful *Smokey Snaps*	2 tablespoonsful *Bakon Bits*

1. Cook, drain and rinse the macaroni. Set aside.

2. Peel the avocado and dice. Sprinkle with lemon juice and set aside.

3. Dice the cucumber and set aside. Mince the spring onions (scallions).

4. In a bowl combine the mayonnaise, minced spring onions (scallions), parsley, vinegar, mustard and seasoning. Mix thoroughly.

5. Add the macaroni, avocado, cucumber and *Smokey Snaps* (*Bakon Bits*). Mix well and serve.

MEXICAN FROSTED CAULIFLOWER SALAD

Imperial (Metric)	American
1 large cauliflower	1 large cauliflower
3 fl oz (90ml) olive oil	1/3 cupful olive oil
3 tablespoonsful cider vinegar	3 tablespoonsful cider vinegar
Pinch garlic salt	Pinch garlic salt
2 avocados	2 avocados
2 large tomatoes	1 medium tomato
1 small onion	1 small onion

1. Trim, wash and cook the cauliflower whole until just tender.

2. Chill the cooked cauliflower.

3. Combine the oil, vinegar, and garlic salt. Set aside.

4. Peel and mash the avocados. Peel and chop the tomatoes. Mince the onion finely.

5. Mix together the mashed avocado, tomato and onion and beat well.

6. Place the cauliflower on a serving plate. Pour the oil and vinegar dressing over it, then cover with the avocado mixture and serve at once.

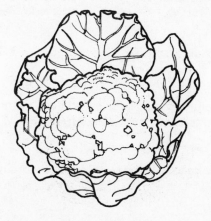

MIDDLE-EASTERN CAULIFLOWER SALAD

Imperial (Metric)	American
1 large cauliflower	1 large cauliflower
2 small avocados	2 small avocados
Juice of ½ lemon	Juice of ½ lemon
4 tablespoonsful tahini	4 tablespoonsful tahini
Lettuce leaves as required	Lettuce leaves as required

1. Trim, wash and cook the cauliflower whole until just tender. Set aside to cool.

2. Mash the avocados. Beat in the lemon juice and then the tahini and mix thoroughly.

3. Line a serving place with lettuce leaves. Place the cauliflower on top and cover with the avocado mixture.

CABBAGE AND AVOCADO PATTIES

Imperial (Metric)	American
½ lb (225g) white cabbage	8 ounces white cabbage
2 avocados	2 avocados
2 oz (50g) sunflower seeds	½ cupful sunflower seeds
2-3 teaspoonsful *Miso-Cup*	2-3 teaspoonsful *Miso-Cup*
4 oz (100g) walnuts	1 cupful English walnuts

1. Grate the cabbage very finely.

2. Mash the avocados and mix with the cabbage.

3. Grind the sunflower seeds finely and add to the cabbage and avocado mixture, along with the *Miso-Cup*.

4. Grind the walnuts finely.

5. Form the avocado and cabbage mixture into patties and coat with the ground walnuts on both sides of each patty.

AVOCADO AND RED PEPPER SALAD

Imperial (Metric)	**American**
4 spring onions	4 scallions
1 large red pepper	1 large red pepper
2 sticks celery	2 stalks celery
2 large avocados	2 large avocados
2 tablespoonsful Vinaigrette Dressing (page 77)	2 tablespoonsful Vinaigrette Dressing (page 77)
2 tablespoonsful *Smokey Snaps*	2 tablespoonsful *Bakon Bits*

1. Mince the spring onions (scallions) and set aside.

2. De-seed and slice the red pepper into thin strips. Slice the celery. Peel and slice the avocados.

3. Arrange avocado, celery and red pepper slices on plates. Sprinkle Vinaigrette, *Smokey Snaps* (*Bakon Bits*) and minced spring onion (scallion) on top.

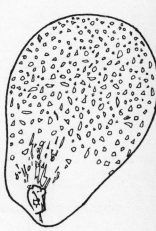

AVOCADO AND COTTAGE CHEESE SALAD

Imperial (Metric)	American
1 clove garlic	1 clove garlic
2 tablespoonsful tomato purée	2 tablespoonsful tomato paste
2 teaspoonsful paprika	2 teaspoonsful paprika
4 tablespoonsful olive oil	4 tablespoonsful olive oil
2 tablespoonsful cider vinegar	2 tablespoonsful cider vinegar
½ lb (225g) cottage cheese *or* tofu cottage cheese (page 10)	1 cupful cottage cheese *or* tofu cottage cheese (page 10)
1 teaspoonful *Tabasco* sauce	1 teaspoonful *Tabasco* sauce
4 boxes mustard and cress	4 boxes mustard and cress
4 avocados	4 avocados

1. Crush the garlic. Combine it with 1 tablespoonful tomato purée (paste), 1 teaspoonful paprika, the oil and the vinegar. Set aside.

2. Combine the cottage cheese with the second tablespoonful tomato purée (paste) and the *Tabasco* sauce. Mix well.

3. Make a bed of cress on four plates.

4. Peel, stone and halve the avocados. Place on top of cress.

5. Pile the cottage cheese mixture on the avocados.

6. Spoon the dressing over the avocados and cress. Sprinkle with the rest of the paprika.

AVOCADO AND POTATO SALAD

Imperial (Metric)	American
1 lb (455g) potatoes	1 pound potatoes
1 small onion	1 small onion
4 oz (115g) black or green olives	1 cupful black or green olives
2 avocados	2 avocados
1 teaspoonful celery salt	1 teaspoonful celery salt
1 tablespoonful minced parsley	1 tablespoonful minced parsley
Vinaigrette Dressing (page 77)	Vinaigrette Dressing (page 77)

1. Cook, cool and dice the potatoes (no need to peel them unless preferred that way).

2. Mince the onion finely. Chop the olives.

3. Peel and dice the avocados.

4. Combine all ingredients, adding Vinaigrette to taste, and mix thoroughly.

FILLED AVOCADO RINGS

Imperial (Metric)	American
6 black olives	6 black olives
1 oz (30g) walnuts	¼ cupful English walnuts
1 spring onion	1 scallion
4 oz (115g) curd cheese, smooth cottage cheese *or* tofu cottage cheese (page 10)	½ cupful curd cheese, smooth cottage cheese *or* tofu cottage cheese (page 10)
Grated rind and juice of 1 small lemon	Grated rind and juice of 1 small lemon
1 teaspoonful curry powder	1 teaspoonful curry powder
Pinch sea salt	Pinch sea salt
Dash cayenne pepper	Dash cayenne pepper
2 avocados	2 avocados
Lettuce leaves as required	Lettuce leaves as required
4 tablespoonsful Vinaigrette Dressing (page 77)	4 tablespoonsful Vinaigrette Dressing (page 77)

1. Mince the olives. Chop the walnuts. Mince the spring onion (scallion).

2. Combine the cheese, walnuts, olives, spring onion (scallion), lemon rind and juice, curry powder and the rest of the seasoning.

3. Peel and halve the avocados. Remove the stones and enlarge the cavities slightly by scooping out a bit of avocado flesh (if immediately coated with lemon juice this can be added to a salad later).

4. Pile the cheese mixture into the avocado halves. Press each pair of halves together. Wrap in tin foil and refrigerate.

5. To serve, cut each avocado crosswise into slices and place on a bed of lettuce. (You may find it easier to slice the rings directly onto the lettuce.)

RICE AND AVOCADO SALAD

Imperial (Metric)	American
¾ lb (340g) long-grain brown rice	2 cupsful long-grain brown rice
2 avocados	2 avocados
3 tomatoes	1 or 2 tomatoes
2 hard-boiled eggs *or*	2 hard-boiled eggs *or*
4 oz (115g) scrambled tofu	½ cupful scrambled tofu
(page 10)	(page 10)
¼ lb (115g) mushrooms	2 cupsful mushrooms
4 tablespoonsful Vinaigrette Dressing	4 tablespoonsful Vinaigrette Dressing
(page 77)	(page 77)

1. Cook the rice until tender and cool.

2. Peel and dice the avocados. Peel and slice the tomatoes. Chop the hard-boiled eggs, if used. Slice the mushrooms.

3. Combine the rice with the avocado, tomato, eggs or tofu and mushrooms.

4. Pour the dressing over this mixture and stir it in gently.

5. Chill the salad in the refrigerator for about an hour before serving.

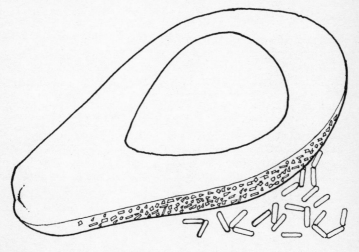

TOSSED GREEN SALAD WITH AVOCADO

Imperial (Metric)	American
1 head crisp lettuce	1 head crisp lettuce
1 large avocado	1 large avocado
A few radishes	A few radishes
2 firm tomatoes	1 firm tomato
¼ cucumber	¼ cucumber
2 oz (55g) button mushrooms	1 cupful mushrooms
2 spring onions	2 scallions
Vinaigrette Dressing as required (page 77)	Vinaigrette Dressing as required (page 77)

1. Tear the lettuce into chunks and place in a large salad bowl.

2. Peel and dice the avocado; thinly slice the radishes; chop the tomatoes; dice the cucumber; chop the mushrooms, and mince the spring onions (scallions). Place in salad bowl.

3. Add enough dressing to moisten, but not drown, the salad and toss gently in order to keep the avocado pieces intact.

6.

AVOCADO AND
FRUIT SALADS

APPLE AND AVOCADO SALAD

Imperial (Metric)	**American**
4 eating apples	4 eating apples
1 large avocado	1 large avocado
Bunch watercress	Bunch watercress
4 oz (115g) salted cashews	1 cupful salted cashews
Vinaigrette Dressing (page 77)	Vinaigrette Dressing (page 77)

1. Core apples but do not peel. Slice thinly.

2. Peel avocado, halve and slice thinly.

3. Chop cashews coarsely.

4. Combine avocado, apple, cashews and watercress and toss in Vinaigrette. Serve at once.

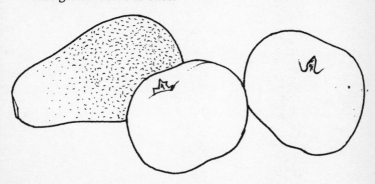

AVOCADO AND ORANGE SALAD

Imperial (Metric)	American
4 small oranges	4 small oranges
Juice of ½ orange	Juice of ½ orange
4 tablespoonsful olive oil	4 tablespoonsful olive oil
Pinch garlic salt	Pinch garlic salt
1 lettuce	1 lettuce
4 small avocados	4 small avocados
4 tablespoonsful desiccated coconut	4 tablespoonsful shredded coconut

1. Peel and slice the oranges.

2. Make up a dressing from orange juice, olive oil and garlic salt.

3. Divide lettuce leaves and place onto four plates.

4. Peel and halve avocados and place on lettuce.

5. Fill and surround with orange slices. Sprinkle dressing and coconut on top. Serve at once.

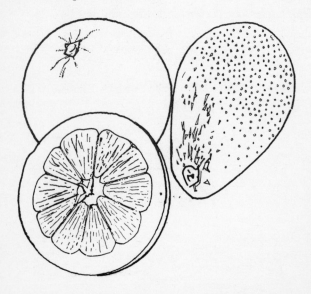

AVOCADO AND PINEAPPLE SALAD

Imperial (Metric)
1 fresh ripe pineapple
2 avocados
Juice of 1 lemon
2 teaspoonsful ground ginger
½ teaspoonful paprika
½ pint (285ml) mayonnaise *or*
   Sun-O-Life dressing
1 lettuce

American
1 fresh ripe pineapple
2 avocados
Juice of 1 lemon
2 teaspoonsful ground ginger
½ teaspoonful paprika
1⅓ cupful mayonnaise *or* eggless
   mayonnaise
1 lettuce

1. Peel the pineapple and cut into cubes.

2. Peel the avocado and cut into cubes.

3. Combine avocado and pineapple cubes and sprinkle with lemon
   juice, ginger and paprika.

4. Fold in mayonnaise gently.

5. Serve on lettuce leaves.

AVOCADO, ORANGE AND GRAPEFRUIT SALAD

Imperial (Metric)	American
1 oz (30g) blanched almonds	¼ cupful blanched almonds
1 oz (30g) pecans (*or* very fresh walnuts)	¼ cupful pecans (*or* very fresh English walnuts)
Juice of 1 lemon	Juice of 1 lemon
2 fl oz (60ml) olive oil	¼ cupful olive oil
Pinch sea salt	Pinch sea salt
Pinch paprika	Pinch paprika
2 large avocados	2 large avocados
2 medium oranges	2 medium oranges
1 grapefruit	1 grapefruit
1 lettuce	1 lettuce

1. Grind the nuts finely. Beat in the lemon juice, olive oil, salt and paprika. Set aside.

2. Peel the avocados and slice lengthwise.

3. Peel the oranges and grapefruit and divide into segments.

4. Arrange the avocado slices and orange and grapefruit segments in a wheel shape on the lettuce leaves.

5. Pour the nut dressing over the salad and serve immediately.

AVOCADO, ORANGE AND CELERY SALAD

Imperial (Metric)
1 clove garlic
Juice of 1 small orange
4 tablespoonsful olive oil
1 teaspoonful thyme
2 large avocados
2 large oranges
3 sticks celery
1 lettuce

American
1 clove garlic
Juice of 1 small orange
4 tablespoonsful olive oil
1 teaspoonful thyme
2 large avocados
2 large oranges
3 stalks celery
1 lettuce

1. Crush the garlic and combine with the orange juice, olive oil and thyme. Set aside.

2. Peel the avocados and slice thinly. Peel the large oranges and divide into segments. Chop the celery coarsely.

3. Combine the above with the dressing in a bowl and leave to marinate for 15-20 minutes.

4. Pile the salad onto lettuce leaves.

AVOCADO, GRAPEFRUIT AND PIMENTO SALAD

Imperial (Metric)	American
1 large grapefruit	1 large grapefruit
2 large avocados	2 large avocados
1 small tin pimentos	1 small can pimentos
1 endive	1 chicory
Vinaigrette Dressing (page 77)	Vinaigrette Dressing (page 77)

1. Peel grapefruit and divide into segments. Peel and slice avocados.

2. Drain tin of pimentos and slice the pimentos.

3. Tear the endive (chicory) into small pieces and arrange on a large plate (or four small plates).

4. Alternate the grapefruit, avocado and pimento slices on the endive (chicory).

5. Sprinkle with vinaigrette and serve immediately.

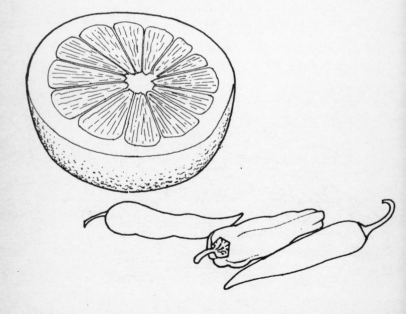

PINEAPPLE, TOMATO AND AVOCADO SALAD

Imperial (Metric)
1 small fresh pineapple
2 large avocados
½ lb (225g) firm ripe tomatoes
Vinaigrette Dressing (page 77)
1 lettuce

American
1 small fresh pineapple
2 large avocados
8 ounces tomatoes
Vinaigrette Dressing (page 77)
1 lettuce

1. Peel and dice the pineapple, discarding the core.

2. Peel and dice the avocados.

3. Peel the tomatoes and cut into quarters.

4. Combine the pineapple, avocado and tomato, and toss in a bowl with the Vinaigrette.

5. Pile on lettuce leaves and serve at once.

TROPICAL SALAD

Imperial (Metric)	American
½ ripe melon	½ ripe melon
1 large ripe mango	1 large ripe mango
1 small fresh pineapple	1 small fresh pineapple
2 medium oranges	2 medium oranges
1 large avocado	1 large avocado
Juice of 1 orange	Juice of 1 orange
1½ teaspoonsful lemon juice	1½ teaspoonsful lemon juice
1 teaspoonful raw cane sugar	1 teaspoonful raw cane sugar
Pinch of sea salt	Pinch of sea salt
1 bunch watercress	1 bunch watercress

1. Cut the melon flesh into small pieces. Peel the mango, pineapple and oranges, and cut into roughly the same size pieces.

2. Mix all the fruit together in a bowl and chill.

3. Peel and mash the avocado. Add the orange and lemon juice and the sugar and salt. Beat well.

4. Remove the fruit from the fridge, surround it with watercress, and top with the avocado mixture.

AVOCADO, GRAPEFRUIT AND APPLE SALAD

Imperial (Metric)	American
1 small grapefruit	1 small grapefruit
2 avocados	2 avocados
2 eating apples	2 eating apples
1 lettuce	1 lettuce
½ lb (225g) cottage cheese *or* tofu cottage cheese (page 10)	1 cupful cottage cheese *or* tofu cottage cheese (page 10)
2 oz (50g) raw cashew nut pieces	½ cupful cashew nut pieces
4 tablespoonsful mayonnaise *or* Sun-O-Life Dressing	4 tablespoonsful mayonnaise *or* eggless mayonnaise
2 tablespoonsful tomato ketchup	2 tablespoonsful tomato catsup

1. Peel the grapefruit and divide into segments.

2. Peel the avocados and slice thinly.

3. Core and slice the apples (unpeeled).

4. Arrange the grapefruit, avocado and apple on the lettuce. Pile the cottage cheese in the centre, and sprinkle with the cashew pieces.

5. Combine the mayonnaise and ketchup and spoon over the salad.

AVOCADO AND PERSIMMON SALAD

Imperial (Metric)	American
2 avocados	2 avocados
1 lettuce	1 lettuce
2 ripe persimmons	2 ripe persimmons

1. Peel and slice the avocados. Arrange on lettuce leaves.

2. Top the avocado slices with spoonfuls of persimmon pulp and serve at once.

Note: The persimmon should be very soft to the touch, rather like an over-ripe tomato.

CHRISTMAS SALAD

Imperial (Metric)	American
4 oz (100g) hazelnuts *or* almonds	1 cupful hazelnuts *or* almonds
Chinese leaves as required	Chinese leaves as required
2 ripe avocados	2 ripe avocados
Lemon juice as required	Lemon juice as required
4 kiwi fruits	4 kiwi fruits
8 fresh lychees	8 fresh lychees
4 tablespoonsful vegetable oil	4 tablespoonsful vegetable oil
1 tablespoonful cider vinegar	1 tablespoonful cider vinegar
Sea salt and freshly ground black pepper to taste	Sea salt and freshly ground black pepper to taste
1 small onion	1 small onion

1. Toast the nuts and set aside.

2. Slice the Chinese leaves to make a bed on a large platter or four individual plates.

3. Peel and cube the avocados, sprinkling with lemon juice at the same time. Arrange on the bed of leaves.

4. Peel and slice the kiwi fruits and arrange with the avocado cubes.

5. Peel the lychees and cut into small pieces. Scatter them amongst the avocado and kiwi fruit.

6. Mix the oil and vinegar together and sprinkle over the salad. Season.

7. Scatter the toasted nuts on top.

8. Mince the onion very finely and scatter over the salad. Serve.

MARINATED AVOCADO AND GRAPEFRUIT SALAD

Imperial (Metric)	American
2 avocados	2 avocados
2 small grapefruit	2 small grapefruit
1 small onion	1 small onion
1 clove garlic	1 clove garlic
Pinch sea salt	Pinch sea salt
Pinch curry powder	Pinch curry powder
Pinch cayenne	Pinch cayenne
4 tablespoonsful olive oil	4 tablespoonsful olive oil
Juice of ½ lemon	Juice of ½ lemon
1 Cos lettuce	1 Romaine lettuce

1. Peel and cube the avocados. Peel the grapefruit and divide into segments.

2. Mince the onion. Crush the garlic.

3. Combine avocado, grapefruit, onion, garlic and seasonings, mix well.

4. Add the olive oil, mix again, then add the lemon juice.

5. Leave to marinate for about an hour.

6. Serve on crisp lettuce leaves.

AVOCADO AND MELON SALAD

Imperial (Metric)
½ melon
1 large avocado
½ cucumber
1 teaspoonful lemon juice
1 teaspoonful dried mint *or*
  1 tablespoonful fresh mint
3 fl oz (90ml) Vinaigrette Dressing
  (page 77)

American
½ melon
1 large avocado
½ cucumber
1 teaspoonful lemon juice
1 teaspoonful dried mint *or* 1
  tablespoonful fresh mint
⅓ cupful Vinaigrette Dressing
  (page 77)

1. De-seed and cube the melon. Peel and dice the avocado. Chop the cucumber finely.

2. Combine all the ingredients, mixing well.

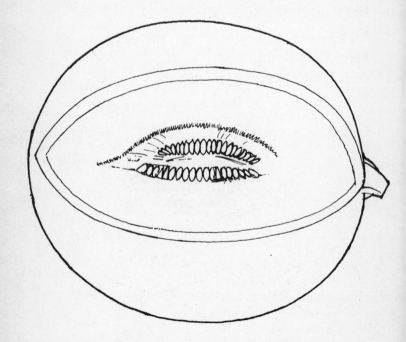

AVOCADO, ORANGE AND BLACK OLIVE SALAD

Imperial (Metric)
3 tablespoonsful lemon juice
3 tablespoonsful olive oil
1 teaspoonful raw cane sugar
Sea salt and freshly ground black
  pepper to taste
4 oranges
2 avocados
4 oz (115g) black olives

American
3 tablespoonsful lemon juice
3 tablespoonsful olive oil
1 teaspoonful raw cane sugar
Sea salt and freshly ground black
  pepper to taste
4 oranges
2 avocados
1 cupful black olives

1. Combine the lemon juice, oil, sugar and seasoning and set aside.

2. Peel the oranges and divide into segments. Arrange on a plate.

3. Peel the avocados and slice into thick wedges. Arrange over orange slices.

4. Chop the olives and sprinkle over the avocado.

5. Spoon the dressing over the salad.

AVOCADO, PEAR AND PINEAPPLE SALAD

Imperial (Metric)
4 ripe pears
4 avocados
½ small fresh pineapple
Lettuce leaves as required
4 tablespoonsful Vinaigrette Dressing
   (page 77)

American
4 ripe pears
4 avocados
½ small fresh pineapple
Lettuce leaves as required
4 tablespoonsful Vinaigrette Dressing
   (page 77)

1. Peel and core the pears. Peel the avocados. Peel the pineapple and discard the core.

2. Dice the avocados, pears and pineapple. Place on a bed of lettuce leaves.

3. Sprinkle with vinaigrette and serve at once.

7.

AVOCADO DRESSINGS

The simplest and most well-known way of serving avocados is to halve
and de-stone them, then fill the centres with a vinaigrette dressing.
The variants of a basic vinaigrette dressing are numerous; here are
just a few. In the following recipes, put all the ingredients into a screw-
top jar and shake vigorously to mix. The quantities given are sufficient
for 4 avocado halves.

VINAIGRETTE DRESSING 1

Imperial (Metric)
1 tablespoonful cider vinegar
3 tablespoonsful olive oil
Sea salt and freshly ground black
    pepper to taste
Pinch of raw cane sugar (optional)

American
1 tablespoonful cider vinegar
3 tablespoonsful olive oil
Sea salt and freshly ground black
    pepper to taste
Pinch of raw cane sugar (optional)

VINAIGRETTE DRESSING 2

Imperial (Metric)
3 tablespoonsful olive oil
1 tablespoonful lemon juice
1/4 teaspoonful dry mustard
Sea salt and freshly ground black
    pepper to taste

American
3 tablespoonsful olive oil
1 tablespoonful lemon juice
1/4 teaspoonful dry mustard
Sea salt and freshly ground black
    pepper to taste

VINAIGRETTE DRESSING 3

Imperial (Metric)
3 tablespoonsful vegetable oil
1½ tablespoonsful cider vinegar
¼ teaspoonful paprika
1 tablespoonful finely minced parsley
1 teaspoonful prepared mustard

American
3 tablespoonsful vegetable oil
1½ tablespoonsful cider vinegar
¼ teaspoonful paprika
1 tablespoonful finely minced parsley
1 teaspoonful prepared mustard

VINAIGRETTE DRESSING 4

Imperial (Metric)
6 tablespoonsful olive oil
3 tablespoonsful cider vinegar
1 tablespoonful lemon juice
1 teaspoonful prepared mustard
Sea salt and freshly ground black
    pepper to taste
1 clove crushed garlic

American
6 tablespoonsful olive oil
3 tablespoonsful cider vinegar
1 tablespoonful lemon juice
1 teaspoonful prepared mustard
Sea salt and freshly ground black
    pepper to taste
1 clove crushed garlic

The following is not a vinaigrette dressing but serves a similar function.

HONEY DRESSING

Imperial (Metric)
¼ pint (140ml) orange juice
2 tablespoonsful lemon juice
2 tablespoonsful honey
¼ pint (140ml) mayonnaise *or*
  Sun-O-Life Dressing
Pinch sea salt
Dash *Tabasco* sauce

American
⅔ cupful orange juice
2 tablespoonsful lemon juice
2 tablespoonsful honey
⅔ cupful mayonnaise *or*
  eggless mayonnaise
Pinch sea salt
Dash *Tabasco* sauce

1. Combine all of the ingredients, and chill.

While the preceding recipes have been dressings for avocados, the following are all tasty dressings for salads using avocados as part of the dressing mix itself.

SIMPLE SALAD DRESSING

Imperial (Metric)
1 clove garlic
1 spring onion
1 avocado
2-4 tablespoonsful milk *or* soya milk
  (page 9)
Sea salt and freshly ground black
  pepper to taste

American
1 clove garlic
1 scallion
1 avocado
2-4 tablespoonsful milk *or* soy milk
  (page 9)
Sea salt and freshly ground black
  pepper to taste

1. Crush the garlic. Mince the spring onion (scallion) very finely.

2. Mash the avocado and mix in the garlic and spring onion (scallion).

3. Stir in enough milk to make a salad dressing consistency and season to taste.

AVOCADO AND MAYONNAISE SALAD DRESSING

Imperial (Metric)
1 avocado
2 spring onions
⅓ pint (200ml) mayonnaise *or*
   Sun-O-Life Dressing
Juice of ½ lemon
1 teaspoonful raw cane sugar
½ teaspoonful garlic salt

American
1 avocado
2 scallions
¾ cupful mayonnaise *or* eggless
   mayonnaise
Juice of ½ lemon
1 teaspoonful raw cane sugar
½ teaspoonful garlic salt

1. Peel and dice the avocado. Mince the spring onions (scallions).

2. Place all the ingredients in a liquidizer and blend thoroughly.

AVOCADO AND YOGURT SALAD DRESSING

Imperial (Metric)
1 avocado
⅓ pint (200ml) yogurt *or* soya
   yogurt (page 10)
1 dessertspoonful soya sauce

American
1 avocado
¾ cupful yogurt *or* soy yogurt (page
   10)
2 teaspoonsful soy sauce

1. Mash the avocado thoroughly.

2. Beat in the yogurt and soya sauce. (Alternatively, this can all be
    done in a liquidizer.)

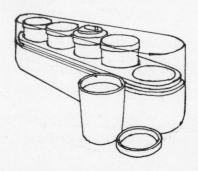

AVOCADO AND TOFU SALAD DRESSING

Imperial (Metric)
1 clove garlic
½-inch (1cm) piece fresh ginger
1 avocado
4 tablespoonsful vegetable oil
2 tablespoonsful chopped parsley
½ lb (225g) firm tofu *or* 1 carton
   silken tofu
Juice of 1 lemon
2 teaspoonsful soya sauce
Water as required

American
1 clove garlic
½-inch piece fresh ginger
1 avocado
4 tablespoonsful vegetable oil
2 tablespoonsful chopped parsley
1 cupful tofu
Juice of 1 lemon
2 teaspoonsful soy sauce
Water as required

1. Mince the garlic and peeled ginger. Peel and dice the avocado.

2. Put all of the ingredients in a liquidizer and blend thoroughly,
    adding enough water to make a dressing the consistency of thin
    mayonnaise.

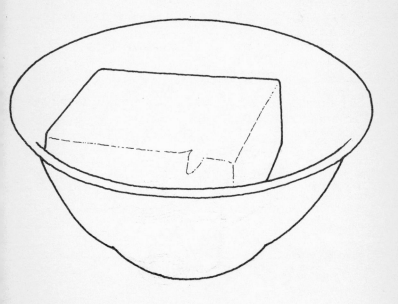

SPICY AVOCADO DRESSING

Imperial (Metric)
2 tablespoonsful cream *or* rich soya
   milk (page 9)
1 tablespoonful lemon juice
Pinch sea salt
1 teaspoonful prepared mustard
Few drops of *Tabasco* sauce
1 large avocado

American
2 tablespoonsful cream *or* rich soy
   milk (page 9)
1 tablespoonful lemon juice
Pinch sea salt
1 teaspoonful prepared mustard
Few drops of *Tabasco* sauce
1 large avocado

1. Combine the cream, lemon juice, salt, mustard and *Tabasco*.

2. Peel and mash the avocado very thoroughly.

3. Combine all the ingredients and beat well.

8.

AVOCADO DESSERTS

AVOCADO AND LEMON SHERBERT

Imperial (Metric)	American
¼ pint (140ml) water	⅔ cupful water
1 teaspoonful agar-agar	1 teaspoonful agar-agar
½ pint (285ml) pineapple juice	1⅓ cupsful pineapple juice
Juice of 1 lemon	Juice of 1 lemon
1 oz (30g) cashew nuts	¼ cupful cashews
6 oz (170g) honey	½ cupful honey
1 avocado	1 avocado

1. Bring the water to the boil, sprinkle in the agar-agar and simmer until dissolved. Set aside.

2. Put the pineapple juice, lemon juice and cashew nuts into the liquidizer and blend thoroughly. Add the honey and agar-agar water and blend again.

3. Peel and dice the avocado and add to the mixture in the liquidizer. Blend thoroughly.

4. Freeze the mixture, stirring occasionally. Try to serve it before it gets too hard; alternatively, remove it from the freezer and keep in the fridge for about 15 minutes before serving.

AVOCADO AND PINEAPPLE WHIP

Imperial (Metric)	American
1 fresh pineapple	1 fresh pineapple
1 avocado	1 avocado
1/3 pint (200ml) water	3/4 cupful water
3 tablespoonsful honey	3 tablespoonsful honey
Juice of 1/2 lemon	Juice of 1/2 lemon

1. Peel and dice the pineapple, discarding the core. Peel and dice the avocado.

2. Place all the ingredients in the liquidizer and blend thoroughly. Serve immediately.

AVOCADO, PINEAPPLE AND GINGER DESSERT

Imperial (Metric)	American
2 avocados	2 avocados
Lemon juice as required	Lemon juice as required
4 slices fresh pineapple	4 slices fresh pineapple
Several small pieces of crystallized stem ginger	Several small pieces of crystallized stem ginger

1. Halve the avocados, remove the stone and sprinkle with lemon juice.

2. Dice the pineapple finely. Mince the ginger.

3. Combine the pineapple and ginger and pile into the avocados.

QUICK AND EASY AVOCADO DESSERT

Imperial (Metric)
3-4 oz (85-115g) Demerara sugar
2 avocados
Juice of ½ lemon

American
½-⅔ cupful Demerara sugar
2 avocados
Juice of ½ lemon

1. Place the sugar in a liquidizer (or coffee grinder) and grind to a fine powder.

2. Peel and dice the avocados.

3. Combine all the ingredients in the liquidizer and blend thoroughly.

AVOCADO AND GOOSEBERRY FOOL

Imperial (Metric)
1 lb (455g) fresh gooseberries
¼ pint (140ml) water
1 avocado
Raw cane sugar to taste
2 oz (50g) plain chocolate

American
1 pound fresh gooseberries
⅔ cupful water
1 avocado
Raw cane sugar to taste
2 ounces semi-sweet chocolate

1. Top and tail the gooseberries.

2. Cook with the water until tender. Cool the gooseberries.

3. Peel and dice the avocado and put in liquidizer with the gooseberries. Blend thoroughly, adding raw sugar to taste.

4. Chill the mixture. Shortly before serving grate the chocolate over the top.

SPICED PLUMS WITH AVOCADO TOPPING

Imperial (Metric)	American
¼ pint (140ml) water	⅔ cupful water
4 oz (115g) raw cane sugar	¾ cupful raw cane sugar
1 large cinnamon stick	1 large cinnamon stick
6 whole cloves	6 whole cloves
1 lb (450g) plums	1 pound plums
1 avocado	1 avocado
1 lemon	1 lemon
1 additional dessertspoonful raw cane sugar	2 additional teaspoonsful raw cane sugar

1. Gently heat the water, sugar, cinnamon and cloves until the sugar has dissolved.

2. Add the plums and simmer until cooked.

3. Cool the plums, then remove the cinnamon and cloves. Chill in the refrigerator.

4. Just before serving, peel and mash the avocado. Grate the lemon rind into it, squeeze the juice of the lemon into it, and finally add the additional sugar. Beat the mixture well.

5. Serve the plums with the avocado topping.

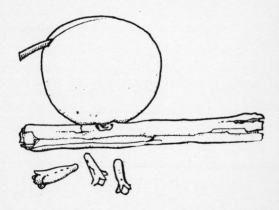

AVOCADO AND SUMMER FRUIT

Imperial (Metric)	American
4 small *or* 2 large avocados	4 small *or* 2 large avocados
Lemon juice as required	Lemon juice as required
1 fresh pineapple	1 fresh pineapple
½ lb (225g) fresh strawberries	8 ounces fresh strawberries
1 fresh peach	1 fresh peach
2 ripe bananas	2 ripe bananas

1. Peel and halve the avocados. Sprinkle with lemon juice.

2. Peel and dice the pineapple. Hull and slice the strawberries. Dice the peach. Slice the bananas.

3. Combine all the fruit and pile into and around the avocado halves. Serve immediately.

AVOCADO, GINGER AND APPLE CRUMBLE

Imperial (Metric)
2 oz (55g) vegetable margarine
3 oz (85g) rolled oats
2 tablespoonsful Demerara sugar
3 large pieces crystallized stem
  ginger
1 avocado
½ pint (285ml) apple purée
¼ pint (140ml) double cream *or*
  imitation cream (page 9)

American
¼ cupful vegetable margarine
¾ cupful rolled oats
2 tablespoonsful Demerara sugar
3 large pieces crystallized stem
  ginger
1 avocado
1⅓ cupsful applesauce
⅔ cupful heavy cream *or* imitation
  cream (page 9)

1. Melt the margarine, add the oats and sugar and mix well.

2. Grease a shallow baking pan and spread the oat mixture on the
    bottom.

3. Place in a moderate oven, 350°F/180°C (Gas Mark 4) for about
    10 minutes, until lightly toasted. Run a fork through the mixture
    and leave to cool.

4. Mince the ginger. Peel and mash the avocado.

5. Combine the avocado, ginger and apple purée (applesauce).

6. Place in a serving dish and top with the oat mixture.

7. Whip the cream and spoon onto the top of the dessert.

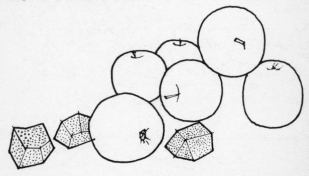

AVOCADO AND LEMON WATER ICE

Imperial (Metric)	American
6 oz (170g) raw cane sugar	1 cupful raw cane sugar
1/3 pint (200ml) water	3/4 cupful water
2 avocados	2 avocados
Juice of 2 lemons	Juice of 2 lemons
Grated rind of 1 lemon	Grated rind of 1 lemon

1. Add the sugar to the water and bring to the boil slowly, then simmer for 5 minutes.

2. Meanwhile, peel and mash the avocados. Add the lemon juice and rind to the mashed avocados, then add the sugar syrup. Mix well.

3. Put in the freezer. Stir once or twice while freezing.

AVOCADO AND BANANA WHIP

Imperial (Metric)	American
2 avocados	2 avocados
4 ripe bananas	4 ripe bananas
2 dessertspoonsful honey	4 teaspoonsful honey
2 dessertspoonsful pineapple juice	4 teaspoonsful pineapple juice

1. Peel and dice avocados. Slice the bananas.

2. Combine all the ingredients in a liquidizer and blend to a thick creamy consistency.

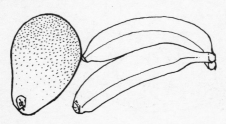

FRESH FRUIT SALAD WITH AVOCADO DRESSING

Imperial (Metric)
1 avocado
1 tablespoonful lemon juice
Pinch sea salt
½ teaspoonful ground ginger
2 tablespoonsful raw cane sugar
⅓ pint (200ml) double cream *or*
   imitation cream (page 9)
Mixture of fresh seasonal fruit

American
1 avocado
1 tablespoonful lemon juice
Pinch sea salt
½ teaspoonful ground ginger
2 tablespoonsful raw cane sugar
¾ cupful heavy cream *or*
   imitation cream (page 9)
Mixture of fresh seasonal fruit

1. Peel and dice the avocado and put in liquidizer.

2. Add lemon juice, salt, ginger and sugar (if using Demerara, grind to a fine powder first), and half the cream. Blend thoroughly.

3. Whip the remainder of the cream and fold in.

4. Chop the fresh fruit and serve topped with avocado dressing.

AVOCADO, COCONUT AND APPLE DESSERT

Imperial (Metric)	American
2 dessert apples	2 dessert apples
Juice of ½ lemon	Juice of ½ lemon
Juice of 1 orange	Juice of 1 orange
2 oz (55g) creamed coconut	¼ cupful creamed coconut
2 oz (55g) stoned dates	⅓ cupful stoned dates
1 oz (30g) walnut pieces	¼ cupful English walnut pieces
1 avocado	1 avocado

1. Peel and chop the apples. Place in liquidizer with lemon and orange juice.

2. Grate the coconut. Chop the dates. Add both to liquidizer along with the walnuts.

3. Peel and chop the avocado. Add to the liquidizer and blend thoroughly.

AVOCADO AND HONEY ICE

Imperial (Metric)	American
2 avocados	2 avocados
Juice of 2 large lemons	Juice of 2 large lemons
4 tablespoonsful honey	4 tablespoonsful honey

1. Peel the avocados. Combine with the lemon juice and honey, either mashing and mixing by hand, or by using the liquidizer.

2. Freeze. This mixture does not usually need stirring nor will it become too hard.

LEMONY AVOCADO FLAN

Imperial (Metric)

1 vegetarian lemon jelly (available at health food stores)

2 small *or* 1 large avocado

⅛ pint (75ml) whipping cream *or* imitation cream (page 9)

¼ lb (100g) vegetarian digestive biscuits

1½ oz (40g) vegetable margarine

A few fresh cherries *or* strawberries (optional)

American

1 vegetarian lemon jello mix

2 small *or* 1 large avocado

⅓ cupful whipping cream *or* imitation cream (page 9)

4 ounces vegetarian Graham crackers

4 tablespoonsful vegetarian margarine

A few fresh cherries *or* strawberries (optional)

1. Prepare the jelly (jello) according to instructions on the packet, but using about a quarter less water than instructed.

2. Mash the avocado. Whip the cream. Add the avocado and cream to the jelly (jello) and beat well. Set aside.

3. Crush the biscuits (crackers). Melt the margarine and add the crumbs, mixing well. Press down firmly onto a flan base.

4. When the avocado and jelly (jello) mixture is nearly set, beat it one more time and then pour it into the flan base. Chill before serving, topped with fruit if desired.

AVOCADO FOOL

Imperial (Metric)	American
¼ pint (150ml) whipping cream *or* imitation cream (page 9)	⅔ cupful whipping cream *or* imitation cream (page 9)
1 teaspoonful finely grated lemon rind	1 teaspoonful finely grated lemon rind
3 tablespoonsful raw sugar	3 tablespoonsful raw sugar
1 large avocado	1 large avocado
1 tablespoonful lemon juice	1 tablespoonful lemon juice

1. Whip the cream and fold in the lemon rind and sugar.

2. Mash the avocado and beat in the lemon juice.

3. Fold the avocado into the cream. Chill before serving.

AVOCADO AND TOFU DESSERT

Imperial (Metric)
¼ lb (115g) vegetarian digestive
 biscuits
1½ oz (45g) vegetable margarine
2 small or 1 large avocado
¾ lb (340g) firm tofu
2 tablespoonsful yogurt or
 soya yogurt (page 10)
2 oz (55g) raw cane sugar
Juice and rind of 1 small lemon

American
4 ounces vegetarian Graham
 crackers
4 tablespoonsful vegetable
 margarine
2 small or 1 large avocado
1½ cupsful firm tofu
2 tablespoonsful yogurt or
 soy yogurt (page 10)
⅓ cupful raw cane sugar
Juice and rind of 1 small lemon

1. Crush the biscuits (crackers). Melt the margarine and mix in the crumbs. Divide the crumbs into four serving dishes and press down well. Chill.

2. Peel the avocado and dice. Put the avocado, tofu, yogurt, sugar, lemon juice and rind into a liquidizer and blend thoroughly, stirring in between time to make certain the ingredients are well mixed.

3. Pour the avocado mixture on top of the crumb base in the four serving dishes. If preferred, chill before serving.

INDEX